With Love to my ~~~~

~~signature~~

July 25, 2009

If God Used Sticky Notes

for Those Who Need a Little Comfort

From: God
To: All

Keep these in your heart!
love,
God

Illustrations and text by

Chris Shea

HARVEST HOUSE PUBLISHERS

EUGENE, OREGON

Scripture quotations are taken from the King James Version of the Bible

Design and production by Garborg Design Works, Savage, Minnesota

If God Used Sticky Notes
for Those Who Need a Little Comfort

Copyright © 2008 by Chris Shea
Lifesighs Cards, PO Box 19446, San Diego, CA 92159

Published by Harvest House Publishers
Eugene, OR 97402
www.harvesthousepublishers.com

ISBN-13: 978-0-7369-2154-1
ISBN 10: 0-7369-2154-0

Printed in China
08 09 10 11 12 13 14 15 16 / LP / 10 9 8 7 6 5 4 3 2 1

For Susan F.
A sure sign that God
both hears and answers prayer.

Where do you think
you'd find one
and what do you think
God might write

if He set out
a few little sticky notes

to comfort you today?

Maybe on the saucer
beneath a cup of tea

It's going to be a good day today!

xo, God

O taste and see that the Lord is good.
Ps. 34:8

or on a well-worn,
best-loved book

on the afghan
on your rocking chair

There, there! It's going to be all right!

love, God

In quietness and in confidence shall be your strength.

Is. 30:15

the mirror in the hall

the notepad by the telephone

the stack of bills to pay

Remember! I have always sent you your Daily Bread! (And I always will... >

love, God

It is your Father's good pleasure to give you the kingdom. Lk. 12:32

or on the
sun-drenched windowsill?

What if we found them
throughout the day,
colorful little pieces of paper
stuck in places we would see

23

reminding us of
God's constancy,
His compassion,
and His care?

A pink one on the coatrack as we grab our coat and scarf

Keep warm today!
You're precious to me,
love,
God

The Lord will
command his loving-
kindness in the
daytime.
Ps. 42:8

a blue one
on the front porch steps
as we set out
for the day

You are Never alone!
Never!!
love,
God

The Lord thy God is
with thee
whithersoever thou
goest.

Jos. 1:9

a yellow one on a magazine
in the hospital waiting room

Even when they have no
words, your prayers get
through to me!
Love,
God.

I will not fail thee.
Jos. 1:5

or a lavender one
on the pillow
for your last thought
of the night.

Of course, if we really think about it

God's sticky notes are all around

because reminders
of His comfort
and His presence in our lives
always seem to find us

wherever we may be

whether smiling in the sunshine

or crying in the rain

little bits of comfort
put here just for us.

A baby's tiny smile
in the middle of a dream

the familiar
and delicious smells
of a home we feel
so safe in

45

the sharing of good neighbors

across a backyard fence

the laughter of children

48

at play on the shore

the comforting touch
of a reassuring hand

resting on our shoulder

every one a sticky note
written not with pen and ink

but written nonetheless
for every heart
upon the earth
to hold on to forever.

From: God
To: Everyone!

Use these for a
little comfort! Keep
them close!
love,
God

Where would I like to see one

and what would I like it to say

if God put a
comforting little sticky note
upon your path today?

I'd like Him to put it on
a down-filled quilt,
one you could wrap yourself up in
to keep so toasty and warm

and I'd like it to say
as only God could,

I love you!

— only God . . .

63

Let my love
surround you today and
every moment!
You are always
enfolded in My
care.   love,
              God

(over →)

P.S. Don't Forget!
"Fear thou not, for I
am with thee;
be not dismayed, for
I am thy God."
            Is. 41:10